D1277888

LITTLE PAPER PLANES

20 ARTISTS REINVENT THE CHILDHOOD CLASSIC

KELLY LYNN JONES

Featuring *PAPER AIRPLANES* by:

ALYSON FOX

JEN RENNINGER

JULIA ROTHMAN

ELISABETH DUNKER

RYAN BERKLEY

JOSH COCHRAN

ASHKAHN SHAHPARNIA

WOLFIE & THE SNEAK

KATE BINGAMAN-BURT

MICHAEL C. HSIUNG

CHRISTINE TILLMAN

CHRISTOPHER DAVID RYAN

HERNÁN PAGANINI

JONATHAN RYAN STORM

BRENDAN MONROE

ASHLEY GOLDBERG & DREW BELL

ALEXIS ANNE MACKENZIE

LISA CONGDON

GEMMA CORRELL

RUSSELL LENG

CHRONICLE BOOKS

SAN FRANCISCO

INTRODUCT

KELLY LYNN JONES

WHEN I THINK ABOUT PAPER PLANES, I am reminded of being

young. As a child, I would enter a daydream world of my own. During these long periods of fantasy, I would draw all over anything in front of me and create sculptures out of whatever was at hand. Paper planes were something that bridged the gap between this make-believe world and reality. They were real tangible objects but represented the possibility that what I imagined could really come to be. I am still in search of my imagined reality. Though a little bit older now, I still want to make something just for the sheer joy of it.

In 2004 I founded the online artists' community Little Paper Planes (Littlepaperplanes.com), one of the first Web-based sources of artist prints. I like to think of the way the site has transmitted work between artists and art-lovers as being like the way a paper plane is used to pass a note in class. And now this book furthers that sense of playful exchange by encouraging collaboration between artist and reader.

Twenty artists from the Little Paper Planes community have been invited to interpret the meaning of a paper plane, creating designs that are construction-worthy and discrete works of art in their own right, whether removed from the pages in this book or not. There is a balance of illustrative and conceptual styles herein that produces a mix of both literal and nonliteral airplanes, all unique to each artist's style of making. While working on this book, it became clear that the concept of the paper plane represented more than just a flying object, but brought up moments of nostalgia for childhood, varying perceptions on the act of making and creativity, and notions around authorship and the collaboration between artist and reader.

Our talented artists have created patterns for their very own versions of paper planes for you to assemble. We have traditional paper airplanes, a shark plane, a plane mobile, and a paper doll–inspired plane, along with an abstract plane, a paper ball that flies (just like

a plane!), plane-esque paper strips, a mini paper house that holds secret notes just like a paper airplane can, and much, much more.

So get some scissors, glue, tape, and string, and allow your imagination to take flight with these little paper planes!

ALYSON FOX

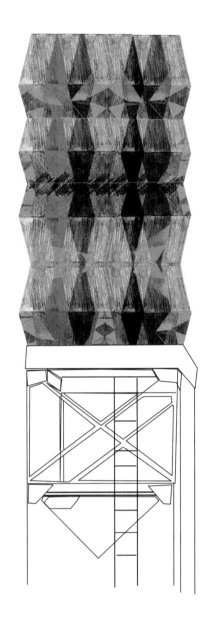

Alyson Fox makes things from paper, fabric, books, ceramics, tape, office supplies, photographs, old tattered things, new polished things, furniture, and plaster. She has degrees in photography and sculpture/installation art. She enjoys designing things for commercial ends and designing things for no end at all. Fox is always working on a handful of drawings and can be seen visiting local thrift stores, hardware stores, and eating chocolate for inspiration. Her work has been published in the *New York Times*, *Nylon*, *Domino*, and *Lucky*, to name a few, and has been shown both nationally and internationally. She designs a small line of limited-edition pieces for purchase under the name "a small collection." Currently she is working on a textile line and a couple commercial projects. She lives and works in Austin, Texas, with her husband and puppy dog, and can also be found at Alysonfox.com.

Paper planes can be vehicles of information, a way to deliver a message. Art also has the ability to convey a thought, an idea, or point of view. How do you approach art? Do you want to convey something specific or do you prefer it to be subjective and let the viewer have his or her own unique relationship with your work?

I always have a story that is going on in my head when I initially sit down to make something, but I also let most of that go once I start working, to see where it takes me. Making work is very exploratory for me. It definitely comes from a very personal place, but I don't overthink anything or else I get stuck. One drawing will influence the next drawing or sculpture, which is why I tend to have a series of work with the same elements.

Sometimes my work is more about composition and other times it's more about storytelling. But the viewer is free to interpret it in his or her own way. I hope to guide the viewer into a feeling but definitely want the viewer to have his or her own relationship to it. That is why all of my drawings of people have no facial features. I think it is easier to step into the work if you don't see a specific identity. I think art is a great vehicle for communicating and can be very specific and also very subjective. Right now I tend to be more on the side of subjective, where the familiar and alarming maintain some kind of delicate balance.

SUPPLIES

Pattern, provided

Envelope

Pen or pencil

Airmail stamp

INSTRUCTIONS

1 Fold along any lines you choose, or not.

2 Throw what you've folded and hope it flies.

3 Experiment.

4 Write a letter to a friend somewhere on it and fly it by airmail.

5 Pattern can also be used to make a swan, boat, or whatever you like.

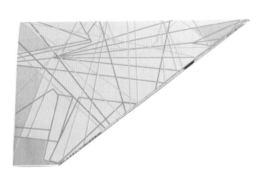

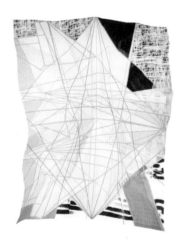

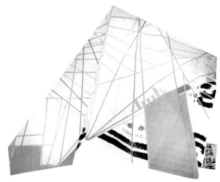

JEN
RENNINGER

Illustrator and artist Jen Renninger has worked as a freelance illustrator for the past decade, creating chic modern images that resonate with a wide range of clients. Her eye-catching work is soft yet powerful, combining sophisticated painting and line work with nostalgic collage materials. The result is a portfolio of work honed to current trends yet rendered with a delicate hand. Renninger's personal work is an extension of the years spent illustrating stories for magazines, with the written word often being the jumping-off point for the image. Nearly all of her work shares text in common and often leans toward phrases and subjects that are inspirational and universal, creating images that linger in memory long after viewed in person. A selection of her client list includes: the *Washington Post*, the *New York Times*, the *Wall Street Journal*, *Harper's*, *Better Homes and Gardens*, Urban Outfitters, Penguin Books, *How* magazine, and Chronicle Books. Learn more at Jenrenninger.com.

The projects in this book rely on the reader "completing" them. Do you feel this is an essential task? What if the reader chooses not to assemble the design you've created?

Since my design consists of three planes that are turned into a small mobile, the construction of the project is fairly important. Each plane has a word, or series of words, on the bottom that spell out a short phrase once assembled. But in the event that someone wants to leave my image as is, I hope that the design will stand up to that choice. I'd be happy to be able to have it fit both choices ideally.

SUPPLIES

Pattern, provided

Scissors

Clear tape

Thin string or thread

A twig, stick, or firm wire about a foot long and at least ¼ inch around

Hook or nail

Double-stick tape

INSTRUCTIONS

1 Cut out the patterns and fold each plane along the lines.

2 Tape the bottom of each plane together so the folds don't fan out.

3 Tie a piece of thread around the center of the twig and suspend from a hook or nail.

4 Tape one end of a length of thread to the center of one of your planes using the double-stick tape. This will both hold the plane together and attach the thread to it.

5 Loosely tie the other end to the twig. Make sure the plane hangs at a length that you're happy with.

6 Continue adding your planes one at a time, attaching them to the twig so it balances and hangs horizontally. Since you loosely tied the thread you will be able to move them back and forth until they are balanced.

*Options:

Consider hanging other things with your plane:

• balls of cotton shaped into clouds

• other words written on strips of paper to add to the phrase on the planes

• small rocks, pebbles, twigs, crystals, or other natural elements

• anything else that inspires you!

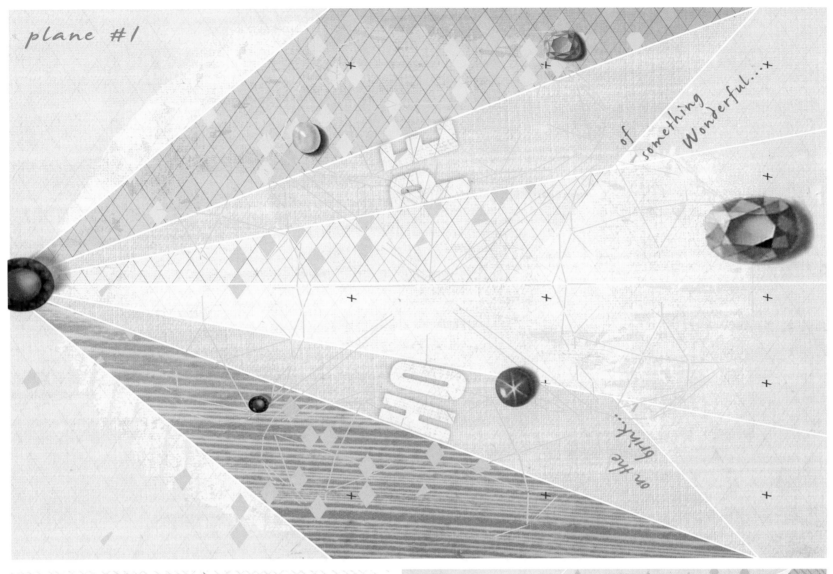

plane #1

of something Wonderful...x

OH

on the brink...

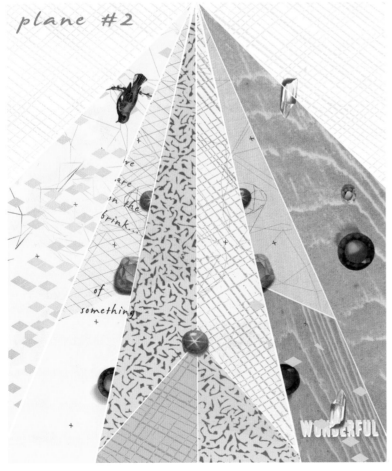

plane #2

we are on the brink... of something

WONDERFUL

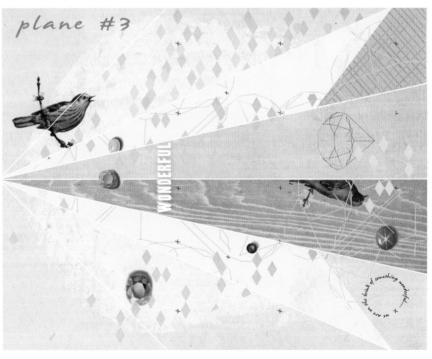

plane #3

WONDERFUL

PAPER PLANE MOBILE

on the brink of something wonderful

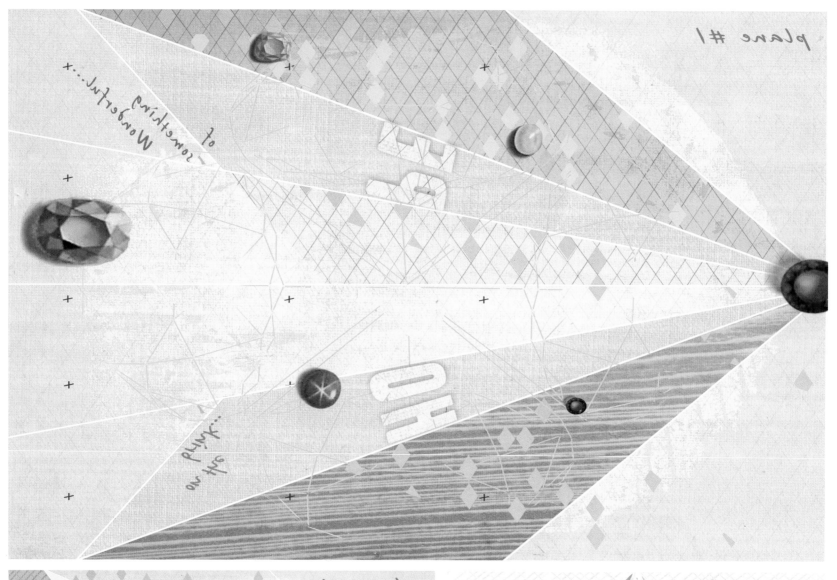

plane #1

plane #2

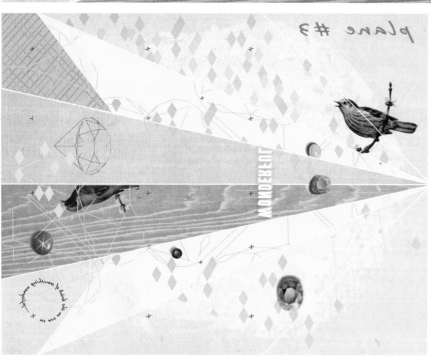

plane #3

PAPER PLANE MOBILE

on the brink of
something wonderful

JULIA ROTHMAN

Living and working in Brooklyn, New York, Julia Rothman spends almost all of her time drawing illustrations and patterns for a range of clients from the *New York Times* to Urban Outfitters. She recently designed a poster for the MTA Arts for Transit, which was displayed throughout the New York City subway system. Rothman is also part of a three-person design firm called ALSO and runs a popular blog called Book By Its Cover. You can learn more about her work at Juliarothman.com.

When did you begin making art? Was there an influential artist who stands out from your youth?

Throughout my childhood I copied drawings I saw around me: characters off of Disney videocassette boxes, my Garfield bedsheets, illustrations from children's books. That's how I began to learn to draw. I didn't think much about the artist on the other side. Sometime in junior high school, my mom took me to a huge Keith Haring exhibition, and I became obsessed with his work. I drew his figures up my bedroom wall with thick Sharpie markers and bought a big clothbound book full of his work. I think he was the first artist I really got interested in, and learning about him helped me understand what art could be.

SUPPLIES

Pattern, provided

Scissors

Needle

String

INSTRUCTIONS

See below.

INSTRUCTIONS

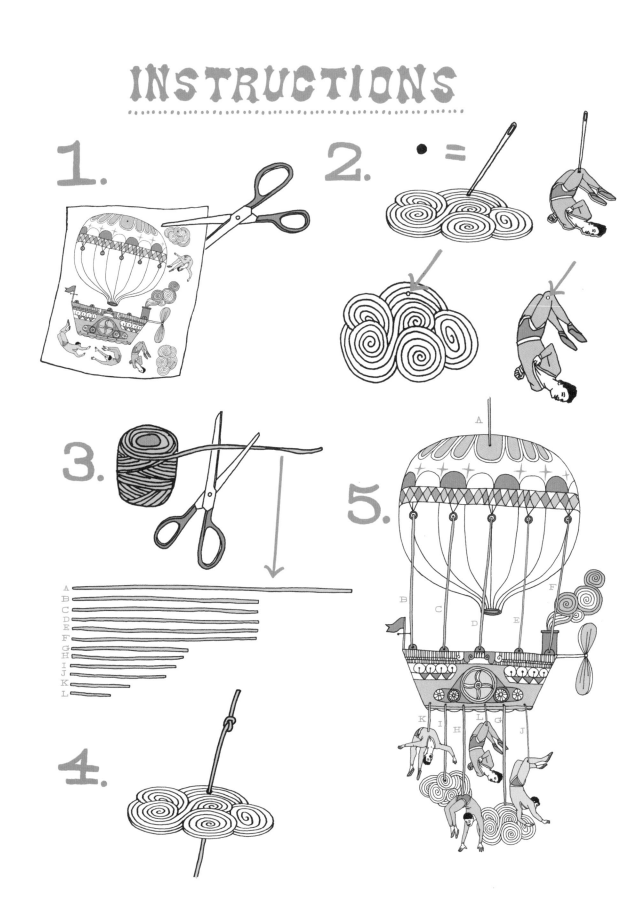

ELISABETH DUNKER

Elisabeth Dunker is an independent cross-disciplined designer/artist. She holds an MFA from HDK–School of Design and Crafts in Gothenburg, Sweden. Dunker also makes a living as a photographer. When working, Dunker enjoys combining illustration, photography, and set design. Learn more at Finelittleday.com.

All children seem to enjoy making paper planes. And they will often rework them several times, refining their design to make it the fastest or fly the greatest distance—pure mechanics. Was that your experience?

To me, a classical paper plane is an aesthetic symbol representing childhood and playfulness. But I cannot remember ever managing to fold a paper plane that looked like a paper plane or that could fly like a paper plane is supposed to—not as a child or an adult. I have too-limited spatial ability.

When I was a kid and someone would fold one of those sheer white paper toys for me, I wouldn't throw it or play with it in that [traditional] way. No, what I did was decorate: I cut holes for windows and doors, and maybe drew some characters to go with it. The planes were often quickly broken in my hands.

SUPPLIES

Pattern, provided

Cardboard (optional)

Scissors

Decorative materials (Paint, pens, pencils, paper, thumbtacks)

String

INSTRUCTIONS

This paper plane doesn't require great origami or folding ability. You can be quite rough and imprecise. I used some old cardboard, acrylic paint, paper, scissors, graphite pen, thumbtacks, and string. Use the pattern as a template if you want (or not), back it with cardboard if you want it to be sturdy, decorate it your way, hang it somewhere, play, and have fun!

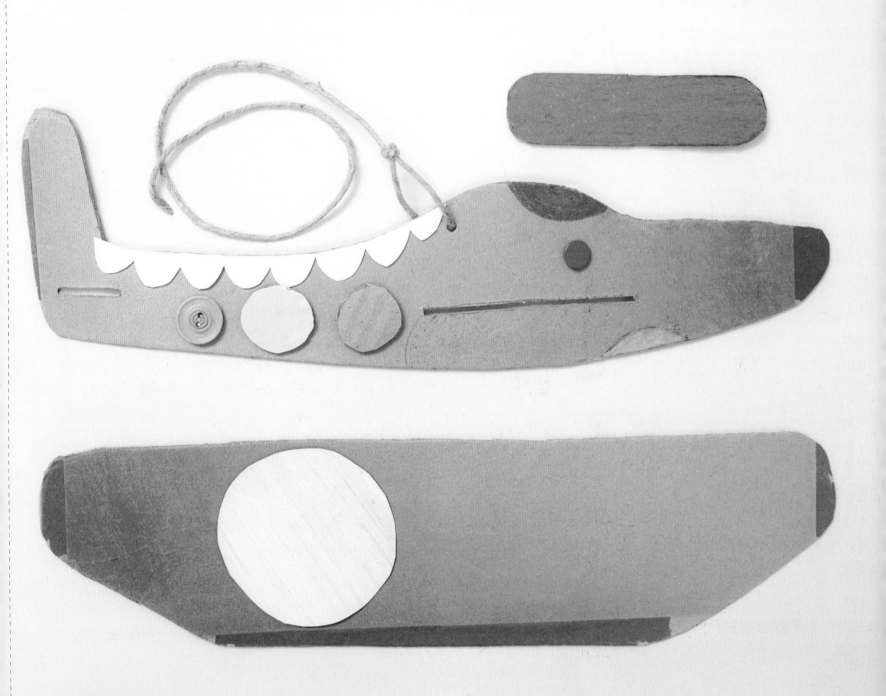

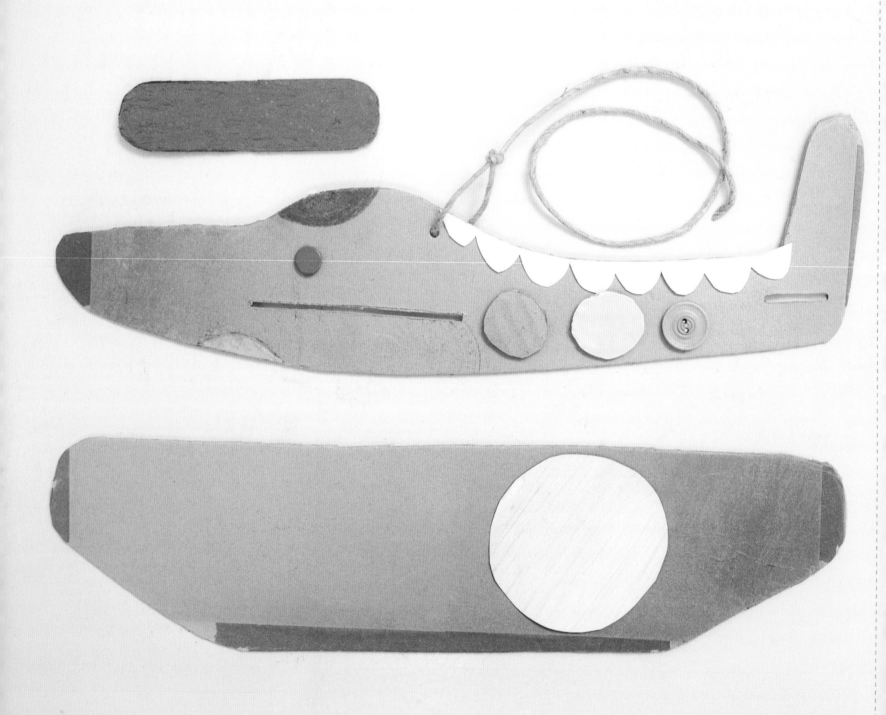

RYAN
BERKLEY

Ryan Berkley creates comic book–inspired art and prints for walls or family photo albums. Perhaps best known for his "Animals in Suits" series, Berkley likes to tackle surreal subject matter in a very friendly way. He works from his home in Portland, Oregon, with his wife, Lucy, and their epileptic dog, Walker.

What does making art mean to you? What's your process when faced with a blank sheet of paper?

To me, making something, specifically an illustration, means creating a piece of art that is intended to be enjoyed forever. It is a piece of my brain that has flowed through my fingers and onto paper. It is meant to be a visual story that should invoke thoughts and feelings to the viewer over and over again.

When I sit before a blank sheet of paper, I visualize something that will be a challenge for me to make into a reality. I create an ambitious image in my mind and do my best to re-create it in a physical depiction. I see a lot of color and a clear concept.

SUPPLIES

Pattern, provided

Bone folder or pen (optional)

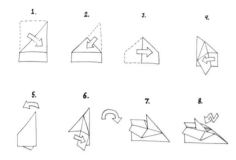

INSTRUCTIONS

If you know my art, you know that I am a huge shark enthusiast. They show up in my work, reading material, TV channels, and daydreams on a daily basis. A few years back I realized that airplanes and jets are essentially flying sharks in design. Look at the blue shark, with its slender body and extra-long fins—it's remarkable how much it resembles a passenger jet. I always had it in my head that I would one day do an art show based on this idea.

Naturally, when given the opportunity to do this project, my mind went straight to sharks. I spent a few hours tinkering with basic paper airplane designs I was familiar with as a kid until I came up with a way to give it a dorsal fin. I was overjoyed! Here you have a great flying plane, with the sleekness and aerodynamics of nature's own underwater airplane. This plane will fly straight, and then either barrel roll or twist in midair and fly upside down, like a shark going into a frenzy!

1 Starting with the eyes of the shark looking up, fold the upper-left corner down, making an even upper-right corner tip.

2 Bring the upper-right tip down across to the left, making a house-shaped page.

3 Fold the page in half from left to right.

4 Fold the left wing down to the left. The greater angle you use, the better the plane will fly.

5 Flip the plane over on its left side.

6 Fold the right wing down to the right, even with the left wing, leaving the fin exposed.

7 Turn plane upright and hold in one hand.

8 With the other hand, push the fin down into the body, creating an "S" fold. This will shorten the fin and increase the plane's stability.

TIPS

Use a bone folder or pen to make your creases straight and crisp. The harder you crease your folds, the more streamlined the plane and its flight will be.

Keep wings bent down toward the body for best flight.

Don't throw the plane hard—a light toss will give you the best results.

Try other versions with different types of wing folds for different results. And of course, create your own shark designs with your favorite art supplies!

For extra effect, why not paint your entire room with an underwater mural while flying this shark?

I wish I had a time machine for the sole purpose of delivering one of these to the eight-year-old Ryan Berkley—I think I would have been his hero. I hope you all have as much fun constructing and flying this as I did.

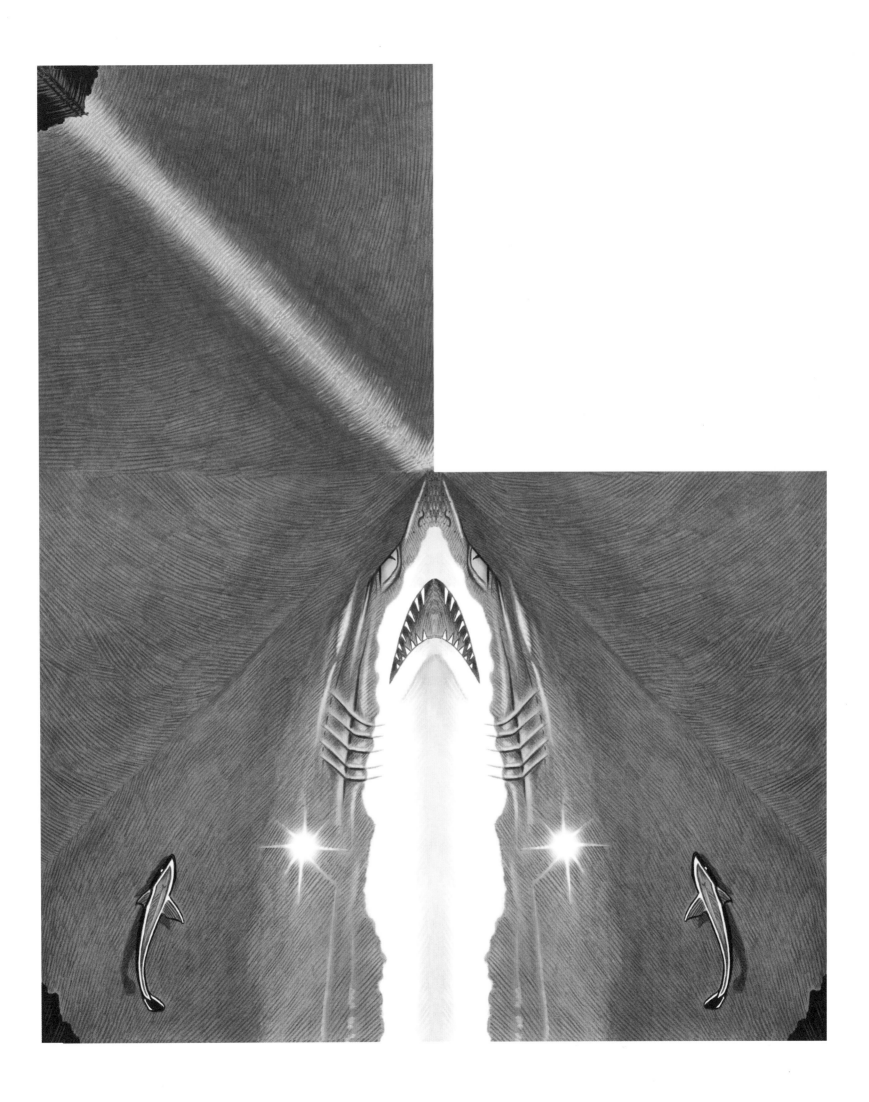

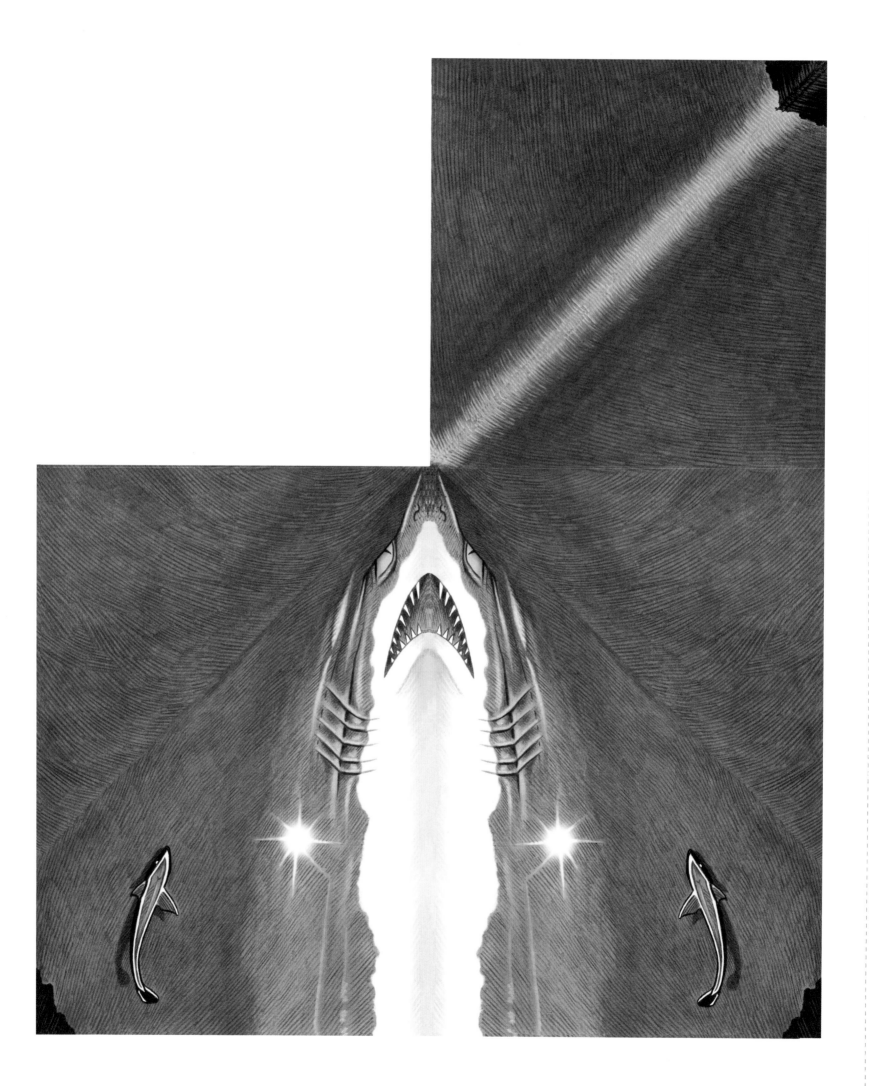

JOSH
COCHRAN

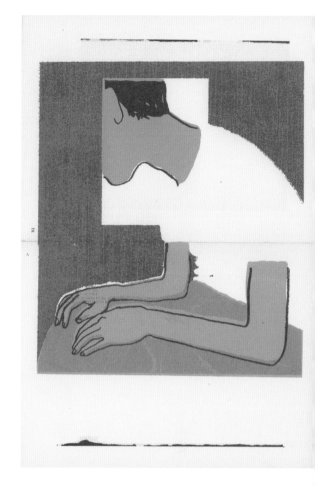

Working from an old pencil factory in Brooklyn, New York, Josh Cochran works for a variety of clients, including the *New Yorker*, Dubai Metro, Criterion Collection, Penguin Books, Facebook, Herman Miller, and Nike. His work combines compulsive lines with a flat graphic sensibility to create a unique world. In 2009, Cochran was recognized by *Print* magazine's "20 Under 30: New Visual Artists" feature and received the ADC Young Guns award. His drawings and silk screens have been shown in galleries across the states as well as abroad. Currently Cochran teaches at the School of Visual Arts in New York. You can visit him at Joshcochran.net.

Making paper planes for the first time is typically a family affair, at least until a child can make one on his or her own. Is there an instance—or a specific project—you recall making with family members when you were a child?

My grandmother is a great paper folder. She would make everything from paper frogs to square paper receptacles to put tiny paper objects in. She made basically everything but paper planes. She's from China, and I've always loved the different approach she's had toward making things from paper. Ten minutes before every meal, my grandma would spend time folding these tiny cubes. She would then pass them out to everyone to be used as a container in which to put chicken bones or food waste or crumpled napkins. When my brother and I were younger, we would wear these little paper cubes on our heads as hats!

SUPPLIES

1 square piece of paper (6" by 6" is a good size; if you want to make a lid, get another piece that is slightly larger)

INSTRUCTIONS

I got so excited remembering the boxes that my grandmother made that I decided to show you how to make them, instead of a more traditional paper plane.

1 Start with a square piece of paper. If you are working with a patterned paper, start with the wrong side up. Fold the paper in half horizontally and then vertically.

2 Fold the four corners of the paper toward the center point.

3 Fold the top and bottom of this square into the center to create these creases and open out again.

4 Open out the top and bottom triangle flaps

5 Fold the sides of the paper into the center. Make sure you fold cleanly and accurately.

6 Fold down the top corner of the paper and then open out again.

7 Fold down in the other direction. You should now have two new diagonal creases.

8 Repeat steps 6 and 7 at the other end of the paper, so you have the new creases at both ends.

9 Open along the creases you just made, at one end of the model. This will cause the top portion of the model to raise vertically.

10 Fold the top of model over into the box.

11 Repeat steps 9 and 10 at the other end of the box . . . and it's finished!

*To make a lid, just make another box, but start with a slightly bigger piece of paper.

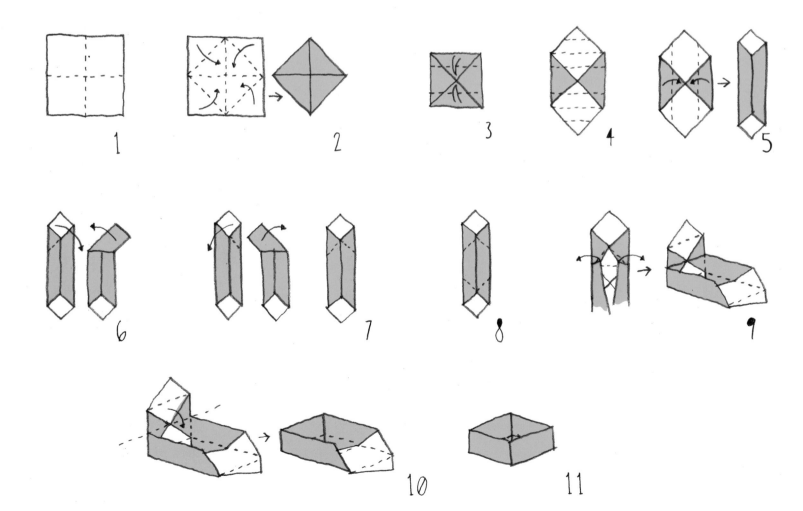

ASHKAHN
SHAHPARNIA

Ashkahn Shahparnia loves beer, brown rice, deep-dish pizza, coconuts, burritos, kale, slobs, slackers, color, collaboration, expensive art, heather, walking, oceans, diamonds, '70s centerfolds, and modern homes in the hills, to name a few. He received his BFA from Otis College of Art and Design. In 2009 he established Ashkahn Shahparnia Studio + Company, and in 2010 he was nominated for *Print* magazine's "20 Under 30: New Visual Artists." He lives and works in the Silverlake neighborhood of Los Angeles, California. You can see more of his work at Ashkahn.com.

Paper planes can be powerful reminders of one's youth, jolting the wielder to a more carefree, simpler time. What's one memory you have of these playthings? And what, if anything, do you do to recapture that youthful sensibility?

Paper planes were way cool when I was in elementary school. I used to throw them around the room to friends and get in trouble. They would usually end up hitting a classmate in the head instead of reaching their destination, though. The teacher would put me outside for a few minutes and then bring me back inside. Nowadays, wandering around town without any plans or goals gives me a feeling similar to those elementary-school days. Wandering for hours and exploring the city is the best inspiration. It's like a big school, and I'm learning all over again. I take photos and come up with ideas along the way, which helps my creative practice and keeps me excited!

SUPPLIES

Any music-playing device

Pattern, provided

Spray adhesive

Cardboard

X-Acto knife (or scissors)

INSTRUCTIONS

Find the song "There Is No Sun" by Jay Reatard.

Turn up your speakers and play it really, really,

really loud. Then . . .

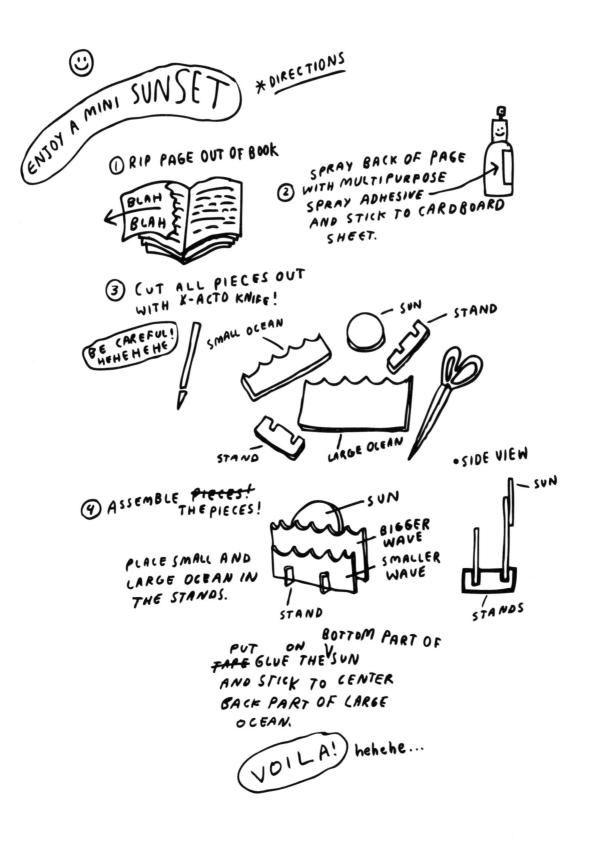

ENJOY A MINI SUNSET *DIRECTIONS

① RIP PAGE OUT OF BOOK

BLAH BLAH

② SPRAY BACK OF PAGE WITH MULTIPURPOSE SPRAY ADHESIVE AND STICK TO CARDBOARD SHEET.

③ CUT ALL PIECES OUT WITH X-ACTO KNIFE!

BE CAREFUL! HEHEHEHE

SMALL OCEAN

SUN

STAND

STAND

LARGE OCEAN

• SIDE VIEW

SUN

④ ASSEMBLE ~~PIECES!~~ THE PIECES!

PLACE SMALL AND LARGE OCEAN IN THE STANDS.

SUN

BIGGER WAVE

SMALLER WAVE

STAND

SUN

STANDS

PUT ON ~~TAPE~~ GLUE THE BOTTOM PART OF ˅ SUN AND STICK TO CENTER BACK PART OF LARGE OCEAN.

VOILA! hehehe...

WOLFIE
& THE
SNEAK

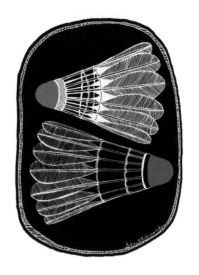

In 2005, Renee Garner and Charles Lybrand met, fell in love, and began a partnership fostering their common passion for creating things. It was then that Wolfie & the Sneak, a collaborative creative powerhouse, was born. Nowadays they are a family of three, who keep their toes in the grass while their laughter tickles the trees. Those are the moments captured through Wolfie & the Sneak goods, which can be seen at Wolfieandthesneak.com/.

The projects in this book are essentially collaborative pieces between the artist and the reader. The artist begins the process and the reader is expected to finish. What happens if the lines of communication fail? Or is the conversation obsolete to the completed plane?

The dialogue between the artist and reader is essential for completing the art piece. In that sense, each image in this book is a separate design with collaborative potential. While our image in this book is a plane in terms of geometry and concept, the paper plane doesn't become an airplane until it is folded, and the airplane is the intention of the artist. With that in mind, though, it's a hard line to cross, feeling free enough to pull the pages out of a book. We've been taught to respect books as valuable objects, complete with cover, binding, and pages intact. Breaking away from that is difficult, and even more so if you think of this book in its entirety as a work of art. We get that, so if people opt out of making the airplanes, we understand. But might we suggest they buy a second copy and have an airplane-making party with friends? That would take the whole thing into an entirely different realm of art!

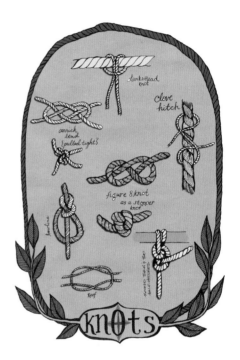

SUPPLIES

Pattern, provided

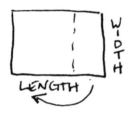

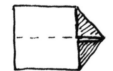

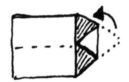

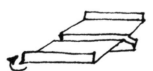

INSTRUCTIONS

This is Charlie's favorite style of paper plane. It makes loopy and unpredictable flights if you throw it gently. If you throw it too hard it just kind of arches up and goes straight down. Think of it as a practice in paper-airplane-throwing restraint, and you'll be quite pleased with the results.

1 Start with the paper length running parallel to your body.

2 Fold it width-wise about a third of the length in. Leave that folded down. We'll call the fold you just made the *nose end*.

3 Fold it length-wise in half and open that fold back up so you have the middle of the length marked from the fold.

4 Fold the corners of the nose end down to make a point at the end of the length-wise fold. Leave those folded and fold the point halfway so you have a blunt end. (The point should now be where the edge of the paper from the nose end meets the middle fold.)

5 Fold again along the middle fold and leave that folded this time.

6 Fold toward you from about an inch up from the middle fold. This will be a wing. Flip the plane over and fold the other side so you have a pair of matching wings.

7 Fold in about an inch from the outermost wing tip to create a wing stabilizer. Repeat on the other side.

8 Gently toss your plane through the air and celebrate its first flight!

KATE BINGAMAN-BURT

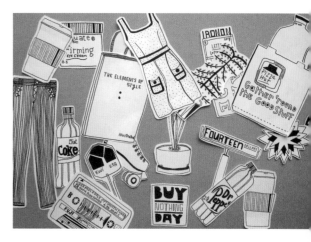

Kate Bingaman-Burt founded Obsessive Consumption in 2002. She makes work about the relationships that we have with objects. Her first book, *Obsessive Consumption: What Did You Buy Today?*, was published by Princeton Architectural Press in April 2010. She lives in Portland, Oregon, where, along with being an assistant professor of graphic design at Portland State University, she also makes piles of work about consumerism: zines! pillows! dresses! drawings! paper chains! photos! She happily draws for other good people too: Target, IDEO, Madewell, Photojojo, *ReadyMade*, and *Newsweek* to name a few. Bingaman-Burt also conducts zine workshops and speaks frequently about inspiration and making and thinking. Check out her Web site at Katebingamanburt.com.

What does it mean to you to make something? What happens when you first look at a blank piece of paper, canvas, et cetera?

Making something new always involves a ton of *process*. It takes me a bit to get into the right mindset, and this is something that I have been struggling with during the last year or so. I feel very fortunate to be busy, but in order to make *new* work, I really need a pause, some silence. This is very hard to come by. To avoid simply rehashing old work, I really need my thoughts to be quiet and organized but still vibrating with excitement for the potential of new ideas and work.

Lots of lists are made. Lots of reading and research. Then I make myself *stop* thinking and then I start making. Overthinking while making isn't a productive action—at least for me it isn't. Thinking and making sometimes are two separate actions for me. When combined, the thinking overpowers the making and then nothing happens. Nothing isn't good.

SUPPLIES

Pattern, provided

Photocopier

Paper

Pencil or pen

INSTRUCTIONS

1 Make photocopies of this plane. Or, better yet, make your own pattern!

2 Fill in the blanks to make your story. Sign the letter or remain anonymous. Up to you.

3 Add extra words, marks, drawings, or any messages that you would like. This is now your plane. Soon it will belong to someone else. What do you want to say?

4 Fold the letter in half the long way and then unfold. Fold both sides as shown.

5 Fold both sides as shown.

6 Fold the piece of paper in half so the inside does not show.

7 Fold both sides as shown.

8 Now take your plane and fly it in a public place. Zoom it out a window of a tall building (or a short building). Toss it down the street (or down a hallway). Let it go out of a car window (or while riding your bike). Wing it free.

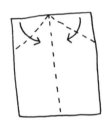

FOLD in HALF the long Way & then UNFOLD. FOLD BOTH Sides as shown ABOVE.

FOLD BOTH SIDES AS SHOWN.

FOLD the piece of paper in half so the inside DOES NOT SHOW.

FLY it in a public Place. Zoom it out a window of a tall BuildiNG. TOSS it down the street. Let it go out a car window. WING it FREE.

FOLD BOTH sides as shown ABOVE.

Fill in the blanks SIGN it OR NOT SIGN it. UP to YOU.

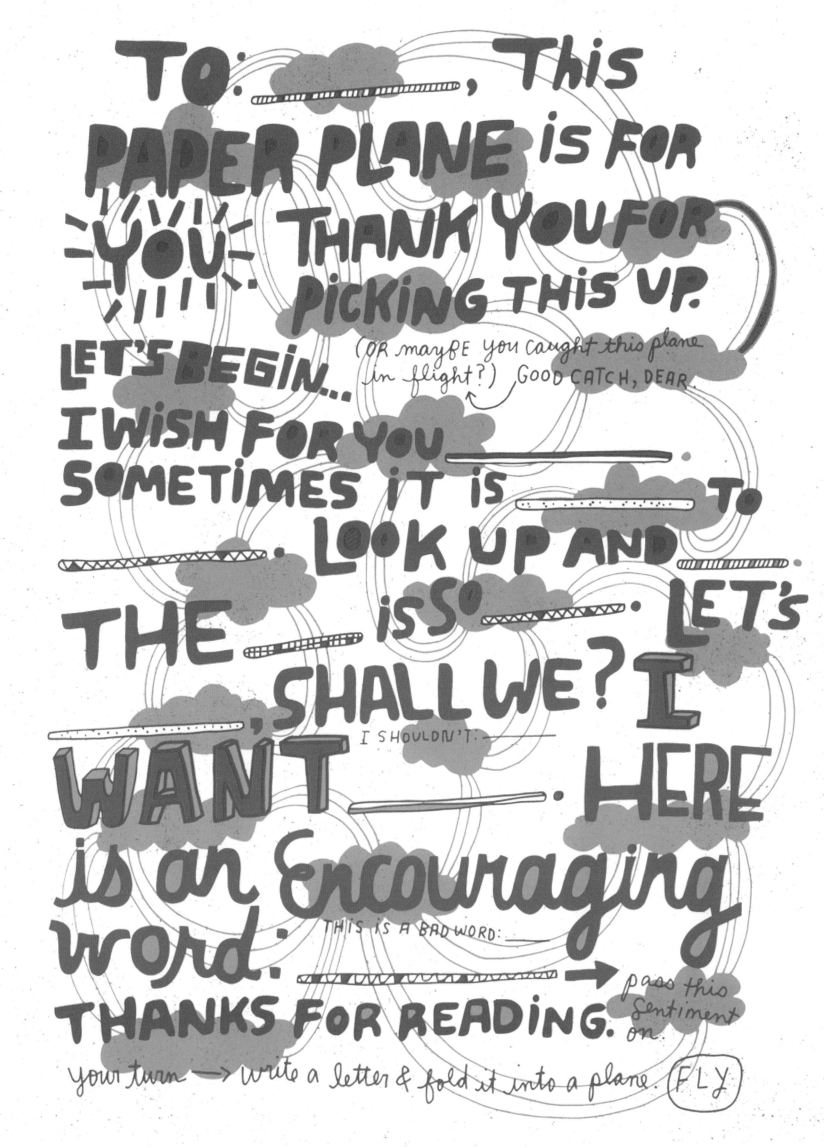

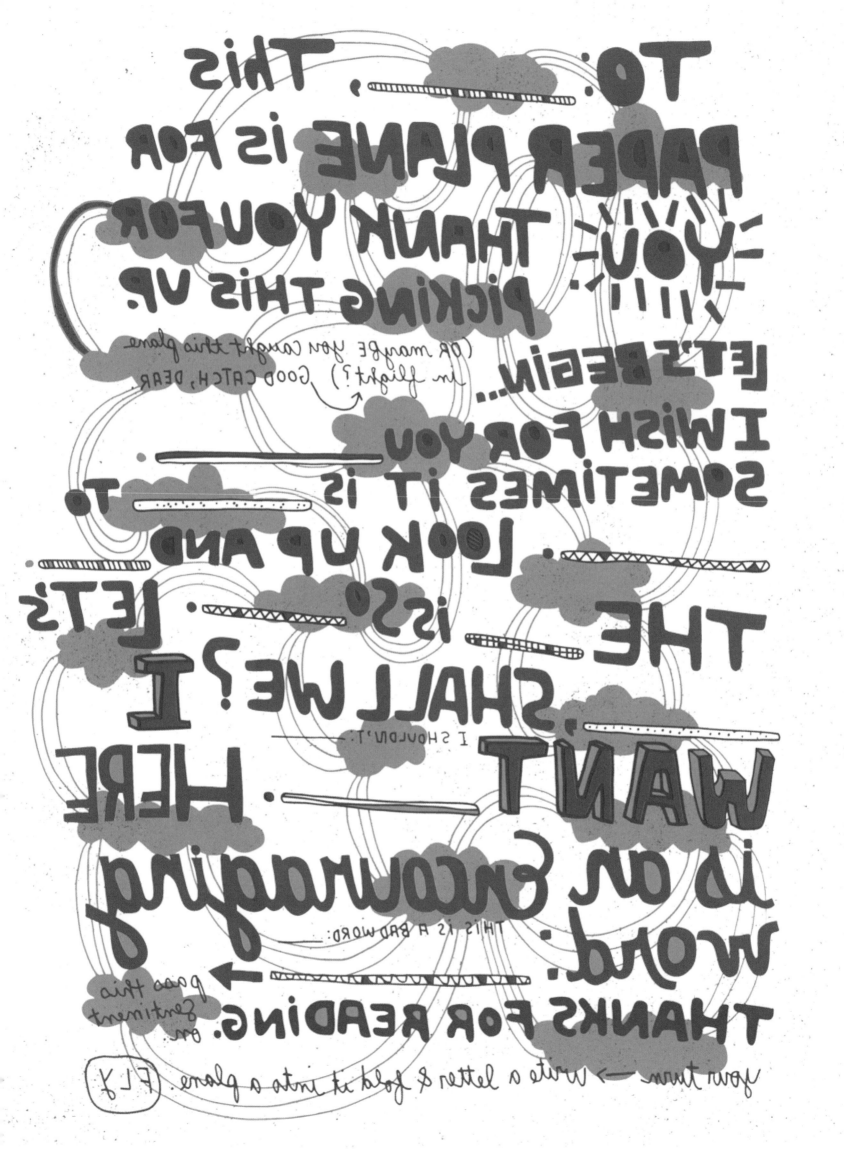

MICHAEL C. HSIUNG

Of Chinese American descent, Michael C. Hsiung is known for his black-and-white ink drawings that depict odd scenes where extremely masculine characters and fantastical and real creatures interact, such as centaurs, bears, and mermen. He currently lives in Los Angeles, California, where he continues to draw, sell prints, and dream about playing Dungeons & Dragons once again. He has done illustrations and artwork for Dr. Martens, Dwindle/Enjoi Skateboards, *Oxford American* magazine, Momentum Wheels, Weekend Snowboards, Matix, and Ambiguous Clothing. He's currently a member of the Human Pyramids Artist Collective, a Vans Art blogger, and an Asian bum with a mustache. His first solo show, *Human Failure*, opened at the Slingluff Gallery in 2011. Read more about Hsiung at Michaelchsiung.com.

How do you approach art? Do you want to convey something specific or do you prefer it to be subjective and let the viewer have their own unique relationship with your work?

I generally try to create in my drawings interactions that are both subjective and specific. Although my characters may resemble real people and/or animals, I encourage the viewer to form his or her own subjective interpretation of how the characters may be interacting with each other and/or the landscape. While I offer titles to inform the viewer, they are also created to mislead, suggest, and remain ambiguous.

Living predominantly in the far reaches of the Schwarzwald (Black Forest) in southwestern Germany, the Wurttern hawk man is a solitary winged creature, although it has been known to hunt in pairs of two or more. With the upper torso of a man, the Wurttern hawk man usually wears an unkempt beard and mustache, an indication of its wildness. Though its disheveled hair appears to be tied up in a "ponytail," the Wurttern hawk man is anything but a cute and domesticated fowl. Equipped with a battle-ax and/or weapons found on old battlefields, this armless but winged beast-man glides through the wooded mountain range in search of unicorns, centuars, and, its favorite, mermen flesh. One known oddity about the Wurttern hawk man is its poor eyesight, usually corrected by eye patches and/or spectacles. If you encounter a Wurttern hawk man in the wild, do not make any sudden motions, for its eyesight is based on movement, like the T. rex in *Jurassic Park*.

SUPPLIES

Pattern, provided

Scissors

Glue stick

X-Acto knife or rusty razor blade

Red pen

INSTRUCTIONS

1 Cut out all shapes: body, wings, leg, and any additional accessories.

2 Apply glue to the underside of the hawk man's body. Fold and press together so that it forms a double-sided body.

3 Using the scissors, make a cut along the dotted lines of the wings where the letter A is indicated.

4 Slide the wings (slit side down) onto hawk man's hot bod.

5 Next, take the X-Acto knife and make a cut along the dotted lines of hawk man's leg, indicated with the letter B.

6 Having cut out the hawk foot, slide it gently through and fold it along the line indicated by the letter C. Then apply glue to the underside of the legs and press them together.

7 Glue on any additional accessories, such as the hawk man's battle-ax to the wing tip and/or hawk man's eye patch to his face.

8 Finally, using a red pen, add your own embellishments, such as blood splatter, to his battle-ax blade.

Do not attempt to fly him.

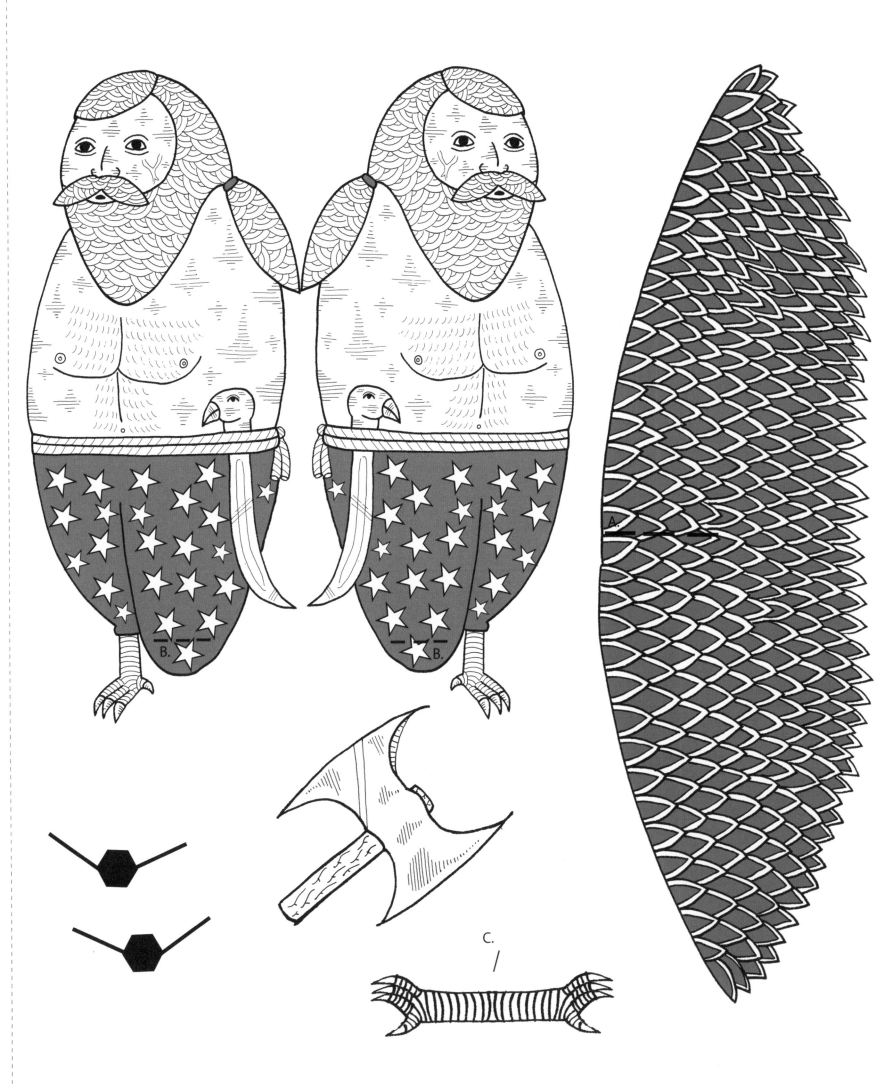

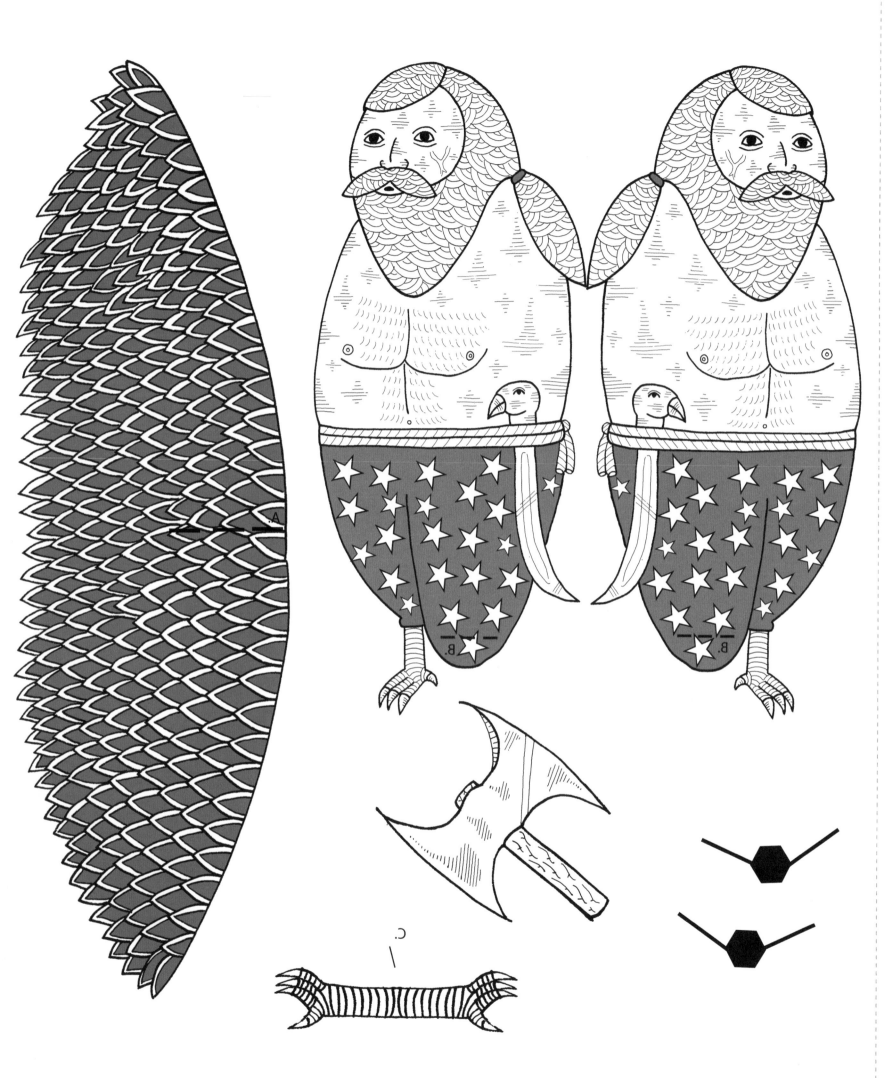

CHRISTINE TILLMAN

Christine Tillman hails from the great northern Chicago suburb of Libertyville, Illinois, home of the Wildcats. She earned her MFA in painting and drawing from the University of Iowa, and her work is included in the Drawing Center Viewing Program and Transformer Flat File. She received a 2010 Maryland State Arts Council Grant for her works on paper.You can discover more about Tillman at Christinebucktontillman.com.

Playing with paper planes seems to have been a universal experience during childhood, usually attached to fond memories. Do you remember the first time you made a paper airplane? When was the last time you played with one?

I could never make those things at all. I should have been able to because it was a fine-motor kind of thing and I was always making stuff. The large motor? Not so much. I've worn glasses since I was four and have had absolutely no success at any kind of sport that involved throwing, balance, or specialized equipment of any kind. So throwing, much less catching, isn't really my thing.

Growing up, my best friend was my next-door neighbor, and her dad was somewhat nerdy. I remember him making paper planes for us to play with. He would crank them out as fast as we could throw them around. We were really little, and so the planes wouldn't last long in our hands. I could never get the hang of throwing them—they'd always just crash down after a few feet. We tried putting paper clips on the front, which was supposed to help. Maybe the plane went a foot farther.

These days I teach at a progressive school outside of Baltimore. It's the kind of place where throwing a paper plane in school isn't an act of rebellion, it's an opportunity to think like an engineer. My classroom is right near a lobby with a two-story-high ceiling. For fun, kids make paper planes and try to get them to land along this one purple architectural beam. Every day I get to walk past the few that have made it. They're kind of hard to spot but I notice. I think they're fantastic.

SUPPLIES

Pattern, provided

INSTRUCTIONS

To contrast the meticulous nature of my faux-needlepoint drawing, my "plane" is made with the exact opposite kind of activity. Just crumple it into a ball! It's easy to toss and probably goes farther than a plane—without perfect craftsmanship.

1 Make sure your workspace is orderly and your hands are clean!

2 Crumple the paper into a ball.

3 There! You did it! High-five!

4 Try throwing overhand.

5 Or try throwing underhand—it may go farther.

6 The vertical toss.

7 The drop.

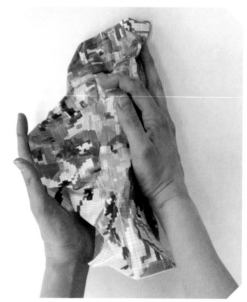

CHRISTOPHER
DAVID RYAN

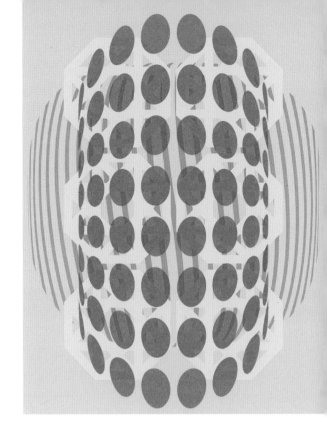

A Texas-born artist, daydreamer, pseudo-scientist, wanna-be astronaut, and untrained intellectual, Christopher David Ryan tends to find inspiration in pretty much anything but especially music, the universe, the human condition, and natural phenomena. Living and working in New York and Portland, Maine, he focuses his creative energy on both analog and digital work. Ryan's client commissions span a variety of industries including work for Victoria's Secret, Kate Spade, Nike, Element skateboards, Graniph, the *New York Times Magazine*, Obedient Sons, and others. Some of his personal projects include Sleepyheads, a line of pillows and printed pieces; *As Overheard in the Back of My Mind,* a series of self-published books; My Little Underground, an online shop that highlights new work quarterly; and his Web site, Cdryan.com.

The collaborative nature of this project suggests that you as the artist create the concept and design, while the reader gives it a new form and meaning. How do you feel about this presumed collaboration, and who's the author in relation to the original and the reproduction?

I actually welcome the idea that the user will bring his or her own preferences and ideas to the table when assembling my piece—so much so that it is this idea that I've based my plane's design around. It's my intention to be the designer of the components that can be used by the reader to create his or her own plane, not to actually design the plane and limit the reader to following my construction. I want to allow some space for a different level of interaction and exploration that the reader would not get with a rigid preconceived design. I will suggest some design options but, ultimately, the reader can configure the components to fit his or her personal ideas. Thus, we share in authorship.

SUPPLIES

Pattern, provided

Scissors

Brain equipped with imagination

Hands

INSTRUCTIONS

The idea behind my plane design is to allow you to completely disregard your established idea of a plane both aesthetically and technologically. The goal is for you to forget how planes look and function and use your imagination to rethink and reconfigure how a plane can appear or even be defined. In this case, for example, a plane may not even need to be a machine that flies. It need not be a machine at all. It may merely be a sculptural object with only the purpose of being admired. The entire experience of creating the plane and establishing its essence and purpose is solely up to your subjective inclinations and whims.

1 Cut out all individual shapes.

2 Utilize the slots in each shape to link them together in the configuration of your choosing. You may use some or all of the shapes.

3 Marvel at your finished piece.

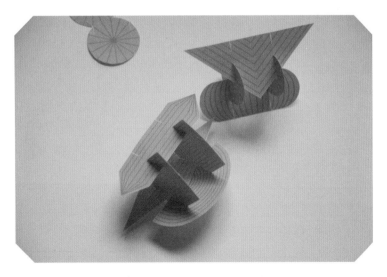
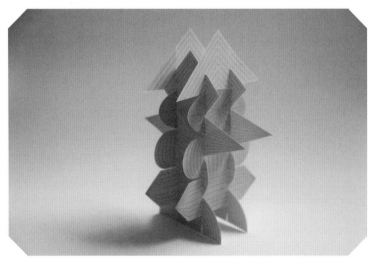

HERNÁN PAGANINI

Hernán Paganini was born in 1982 in the little town of Zárate, Buenos Aires, Argentina. A graphic designer at the public University of Buenos Aires, where he's been teaching morphology since 2003, he also develops workshops for children and designers. You can experience his work via Hernanpaganini.com.ar.

Some artists, in looking back on their growing-up years, came to realize that making a paper airplane was their first experience making "art." What was your earliest act of creating "art"?

When I was six I hid a can in my closet for two years. From time to time I added a bit of different perfumes that I stole from the bathroom of my house. In those days I dreamed of being able to generate a unique and delicious fragrance. I was excited to connect with the can, watching it change over time as if it were magic. I love experimenting with the elements that surround us every day. I have this need to preserve a memory as well as a fascination with the unknown.

SUPPLIES

Pattern, provided

Spanish-English dictionary (optional)

Scissors

INSTRUCTIONS

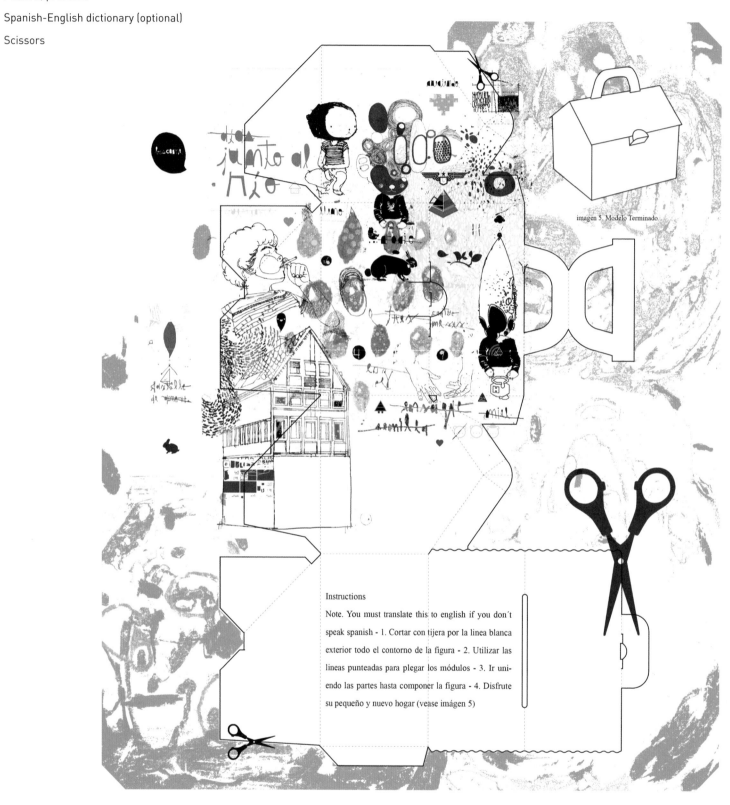

imagen 5. Modelo Terminado

Instructions

Note. You must translate this to english if you don´t speak spanish - 1. Cortar con tijera por la linea blanca exterior todo el contorno de la figura - 2. Utilizar las lineas punteadas para plegar los módulos - 3. Ir uniendo las partes hasta componer la figura - 4. Disfrute su pequeño y nuevo hogar (vease imágen 5)

JONATHAN RYAN STORM

Jonathan Ryan Storm was born in Phoenix, Arizona, in 1980, and grew up in California, Illinois, Texas, and London. He creates a variety of work, including paintings, collages, and detailed line drawings and illustrations. His work has been exhibited internationally, from Seattle to Copenhagen. He has also designed album covers for various artists on the Moorworks and Autumn Records labels. Storm currently lives and works in Brattleboro, Vermont, and you can also find him at Jonathanryanstorm.com.

What does it mean to you to create something? What happens when you first look at a blank canvas, and where do you find inspiration?

To me, "to make something" means "to keep living." When I first look at a blank piece of paper, all I see is its blankness. Hopefully after a while something jumps out, then I go to work. I usually only start making something once an idea comes into my head—a square, a line, a mound. I'll draw from time to time in a sketchbook, and sometimes little pieces turn into big pieces. It's all a mystery. I mainly have no idea how it works.

SUPPLIES

Pattern, provided

Scissors

INSTRUCTIONS

Cut along dotted line. Patiently wad into a ball.

Find a tall building and a sunny day. Toss.

BRENDAN MONROE

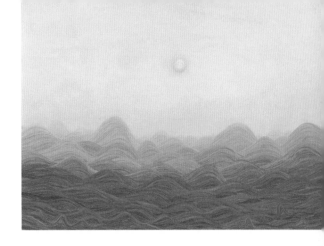

Californian Brendan Monroe is someone who is curious about the way things work. His artwork is half inspired by science and half by speculations on dreams. His paintings are filled with blood cells, misshapen globs, and, once in a while, hydrogen atoms. Monroe invents imagined mindscapes and sculpts inquisitive wooden figures. Based in Sweden, his work can also be found online at Brendanmonroe.com.

Paper planes are often identified as a young person's first art project, especially considering how transformative the act of turning a 2-D blank piece of paper into a 3-D flying object is. At what age did you begin making "art"? When did you decide you wanted to be an artist?

I don't think I ever wanted to be an artist when I was young. I didn't even think of it as something that someone could be until college. I do remember making art for art's sake when I was young, though. I'm not sure why I did it except that I enjoyed it. At one point I even started to get paid for it from my dad. He used to pay $1 for a drawing. That was probably when I was nine or ten. I have memories of switching between that and trimming the bougainvillea to earn some money to go to 7-Eleven and buy candy.

SUPPLIES

Pattern, provided

INSTRUCTIONS

This plane traveling through the air nearing the speed of light will experience time at a slower rate than the person who threw it. This is part of Einstein's theory of relativity, known as *time dilation*. If you placed a clock on this plane and then threw it at its fastest possible speed, that clock would move just a tiny bit slower when compared to another clock that stayed stationary. This plane is designed for speed.

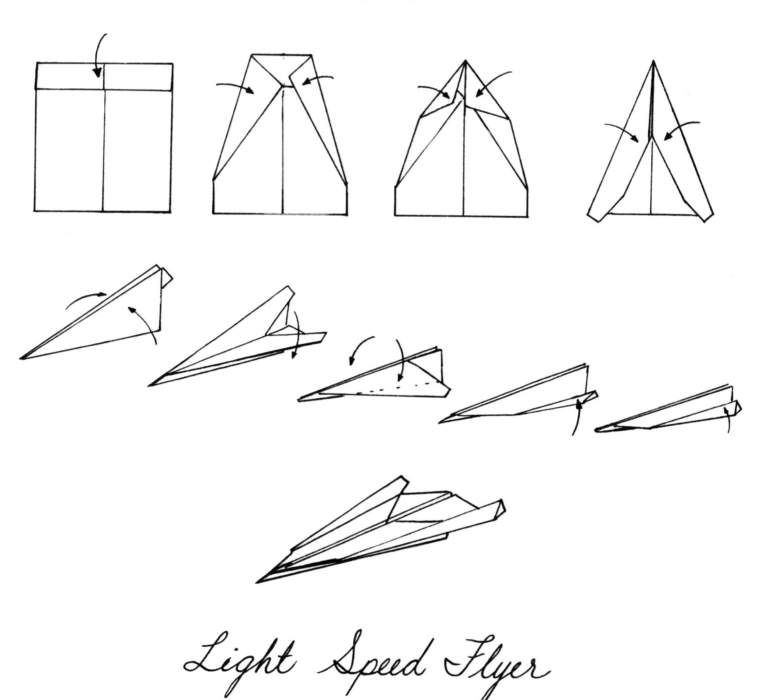

Light Speed Flyer

ASHLEY GOLDBERG & DREW BELL

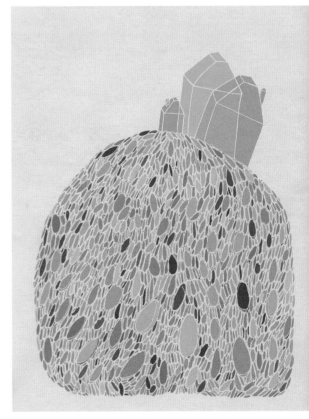

Ashley Goldberg and Drew Bell are creative partners in crime, living and loving in Portland, Oregon. They live with Isadora the cat and mounds of shipping supplies. Ashley says, "I have loved arts, crafts, creatures, and nature my entire life. I enjoy focusing on portraiture and capturing a brief moment in time. My artwork tends to be simple, but with a sophisticated or stark color palette. I believe great emotion can be conveyed in a simple gesture or look. The characters we create, whether monsters or little girls, are simple, humorous, empathetic, and a little bit pathetic." They have been featured by Inc., DIY, the *New York Times*, Urban Outfitters, American Greetings, and many more. Visit them online at Ashleyganddrew.com.

This project brings up questions around authorship. You as the artist create the concept and design, however once assembled by the reader it can be something entirely different. The reader can follow your directions to a tee or dismiss them and approach your piece his or her way. So in the end, who gets to decide how it's used? Who's the owner?

I think this is a bit of a tough question to answer. If it were a print or painting I have a clear answer: You can display the piece or not display the piece. I mean, sure, you can cut it up, make a hat of it,

et cetera, but that is not likely to happen. So my only concern with the art I usually sell is whether someone is getting personal use and enjoyment from it or if he or she is using it in some way for profit—putting my images on bags, clothing, or posters. So there is a clear right or wrong here. Yes, the customer owns the *piece*, but the artist maintains ownership of all the *rights*. Copyright and ethics 101.

When the piece I create becomes a collaboration with the consumer, the authorship and ownership change. For instance, when someone asks for permission to use one of my pieces for a tattoo, and he or she is thinking of adding something or taking something away or changing the colors, I am always shocked when asked if that is okay. Is it okay? *Of course!* It is *your* body! In that case I think the consumer—or viewer, user . . . whichever the best term may be, and sometimes all are applicable—trumps the artist. The ownership of it being on their body makes it more theirs then mine. If someone said, "I love your tattoo," I would expect the person to say, "Thanks!" and take it primarily as a compliment to himself, rather than a compliment to the tattoo artist and a compliment to me.

Now with the designing of a paper plane: I am completely content with the idea of the reader doing anything he or she wants with it as long

as it's not for profit. I think it's a split of ownership, but the percentage changes depending on what's done with it. If the reader follows the instructions to a tee, I think the ownership is pretty much halfsies, with each side probably feeling like they have a bit more ownership of it than the other. The artist thinks, "Well, I did *design* it . . ." and the reader thinks, "Well, I did *make* it." *But* if the reader took the instructions and modified the plane or turned it into something else altogether, like folded it into a paper crane instead of a plane, or used the page for the cover of a self-made book, then I think my art becomes more background noise to their design and concept, and therefore the scales tip more heavily in favor of the reader.

SUPPLIES

Pattern, provided

Scissors

An unsuspecting recipient

INSTRUCTIONS

1 Fold the short end to the long end to make a triangle.

2 Fold the triangle in half toward the excess.

3 Fold this shape in half.

4 Fold the square corner into a wee triangle. Unfold the plane and turn this wee triangle inside out.

5 Fold the wing edges back to meet the bottom edge.

6 Heart attack!

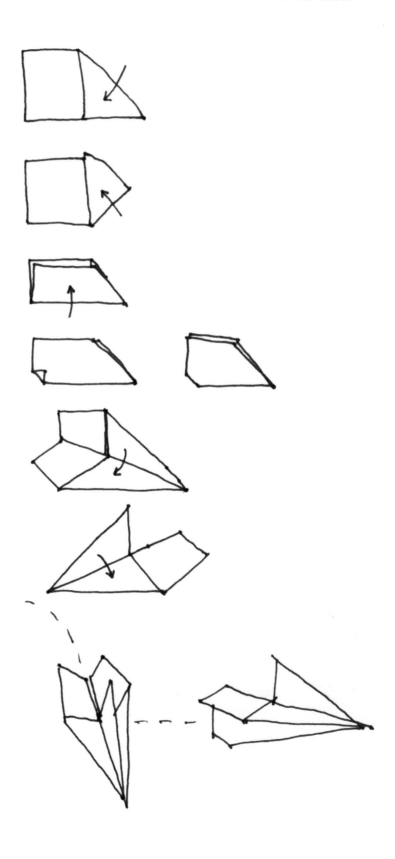

ALEXIS ANNE
MACKENZIE

Alexis Anne Mackenzie was born and raised in the Midwest, and attended Tufts University/ School of the Museum of Fine Arts in Boston, where she earned her BFA. She has resided in San Francisco since 2004. Her collage work has been featured in galleries and publications around the world, including solo shows in San Francisco, Chicago, and Los Angeles. More of Mackenzie's art can be seen at Alexisanne.com.

Paper planes often represent playfulness; they are something most people have made at some point in their life. What do you associate with when thinking about a paper plane? What memories come to mind?

When I think of making paper planes, it's hard for me to recall a specific moment, but I remember learning to fold origami shapes and cut patterns into paper snowflakes, and discovering the magic there was in manipulating a flat sheet of paper into something else altogether. That's really when I learned that paper is a kind of living thing, capable of being and becoming many other things. The amorphous capabilities I discovered in paper at that age are certainly what kept me coming back to it over the years. I still love manipulating paper into new shapes and representations in my collage work.

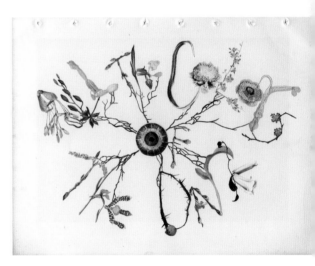

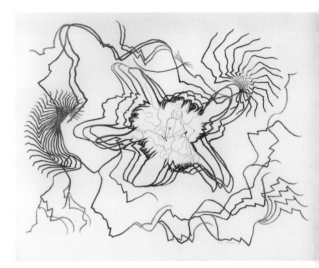

SUPPLIES

Pattern, provided

INSTRUCTIONS

1 Punch out the full page from this book.

2 Spend a few moments with the sheet, considering the layers, depths, intricacies, twists, turns, parallels, et cetera represented upon it, and how you relate to these things.

3 Proceed to shred the page into as many tiny pieces as you can, using only your fingers, and fling them into the air.

LISA
CONGDON

San Francisco illustrator and fine artist Lisa Congdon was raised in both upstate New York and Northern California, where she grew to love the mountains, trees, and animals that surrounded her. That love is now expressed most intensely through her paintings and drawings. Congdon lives and works in the Mission District of San Francisco, where you can often find her walking her Chihuahua, Wilfredo, or riding her bike. Or you can find her at Lisacongdon.com.

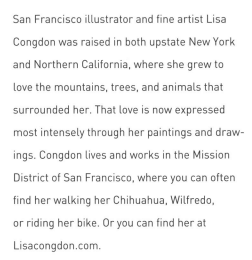

Art tells a visual story. Does that end purpose change depending on whether you're creating for yourself or a client? What do you find more enjoyable?

There is a huge difference between my personal work and my illustration work in terms of messaging. There are exceptions, but for the most part, illustration is by definition art that portrays a specific idea or point of view; in many cases in my illustration work I am drawing or painting the ideas of other people—their stories, their perspectives, even their aesthetic! So in my personal work I tend to prefer a much more subjective approach—that is, to create interesting narrative scenes that allow the viewer to create their own stories. I find this kind of work much more satisfying.

SUPPLIES

Pattern pieces, provided (for each plane, one each of the fuselage, wing, and tail)

Scissors or X-Acto knife

Paper clip

Glue stick (optional)

Thin balsa wood (optional)

INSTRUCTIONS

When I was a kid, I loved playing with things that were really concrete (had parameters and boundaries) and also allowed for choice within those constraints. It might have had something to do with being a creative kid: I liked and appreciated the boundaries but also had to have some creative choices. As part of this project, I thought about paper things that I played with as a child. While I did play quite a bit with paper planes (and loved making gliders in particular), and played around a bit with origami, I really loved paper dolls. What I loved about them were the extensive combinations of clothing, hats, and shoes with which you could adorn your paper doll. If you made your own paper doll and clothing, your options were truly endless. I wanted to design a paper plane that was like a paper doll: The construction and assembly are straightforward, but there are multiple design and color options for the user to experience.

1 Cut out the fuselage pieces.

2 Cut the two slots out of the fuselages for the wings and tail.

3 Cut out the wings and tail.

4 Slide the wing and tail into the fuselage so that they are as centered as possible.

5 Choose coordinating patterns to make your gliders look exactly the way you'd like. Mix and match different patterned fuselages, wings, and tails for a variety of pretty gliders.

6 Throw the planes. The glider may stall and take a nosedive. If so, you might add some ballast to the nose of the fuselage. To do this you can fasten a paper clip to it. Also, if the plane is too limp because the paper is too thin, glue the glider parts (fuselage, wing, and tail) to balsa wood with a glue stick for a sturdier plane.

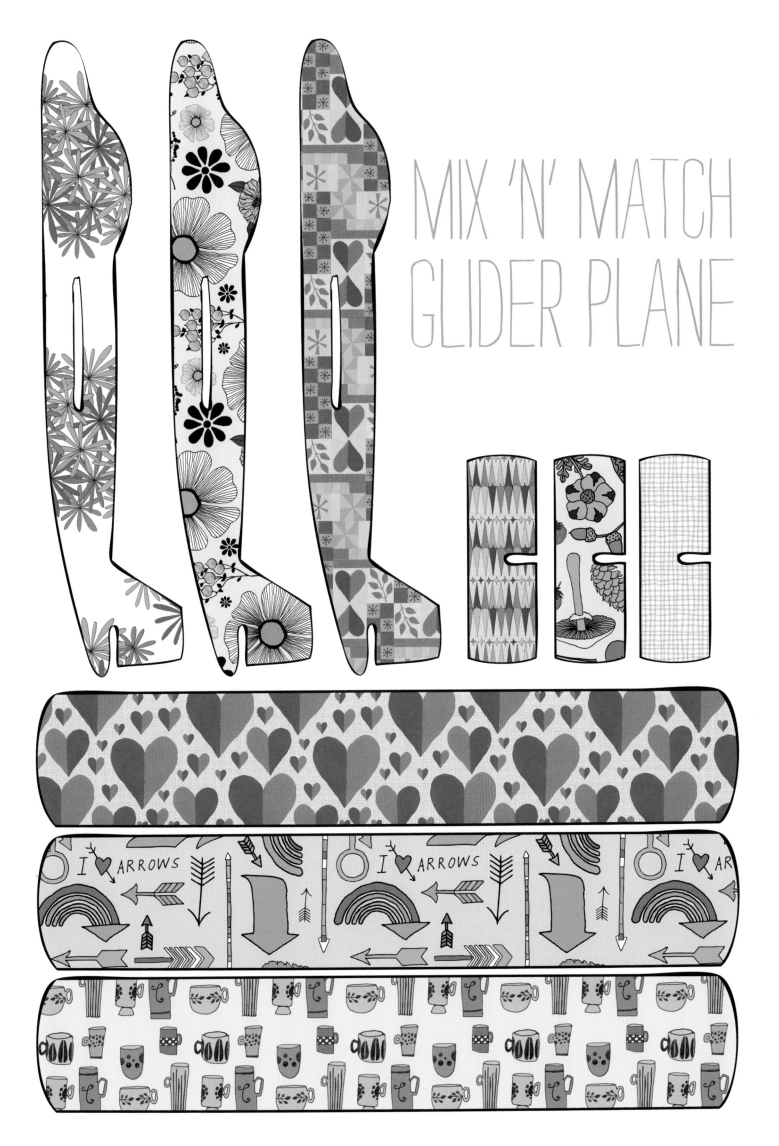

MIX 'N' MATCH
GLIDER PLANE

MIX 'N' MATCH
GLIDER PLANE

GEMMA CORRELL

I LIKE YOU.

Thanks to the wonders of spectacle technology, Gemma Correll manages to hold down a full-time job as a freelance illustrator, despite her poor eyesight. She bumps into things only occasionally. Correll currently lives with her Pug, Mr. Pickles, in Berlin, Germany, where she enjoys drinking good coffee and frequenting the flea markets. You can see her work at Gemmacorrell.com.

When a reader uses this book to make a plane, there is an inherent dialogue between the artist and the reader. The expectation is that the reader will complete the project . . . but maybe not. Is it important that your 2-D piece be transformed into a 3-D object by the reader exactly as you've intended?

The reader definitely plays an important role in completing the project, and I hope that he or she will cut and assemble my piece, because I've designed it with the specific intention that it will be folded and used, taken beyond the flat page. I enjoy working with narrative forms, so this is an interesting facet of that. I feel like I've started the dialogue for the reader to interpret and continue as they wish. I don't care how it's assembled or folded or used, but I like the fact that it's going beyond the flat, printed page.

SUPPLIES

Pattern, provided

Scissors

Tape (or glue or stapler—depending on how you want the wings attached)

INSTRUCTIONS

Turn your beloved pet into a flying machine with this handy cut-out kit. Simply cut the band to the desired length, secure around your pet's middle, and attach the wings on either side. . . . Fasten your seatbelts; we're ready for takeoff!

Optional extra accessories for your pet: flying goggles, pilot hat, jaunty scarf, et cetera.

If your pet is plumper than the waistband of paper in the pattern will allow for, you can add extra paper to extend it.

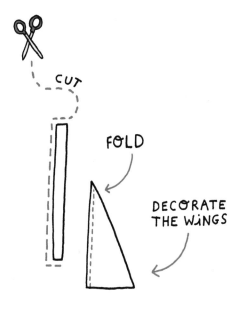

PET AIR DOES NOT ACCEPT ANY RESPONSIBILITY FOR DELAYS DUE TO DISTRACTION BY: CAT-NIP TOYS, tAIL CHASING, OR NIBBLING OF tHE AIRCRAFT'S WINGS.

HAVE A gREAT FLIGHt!

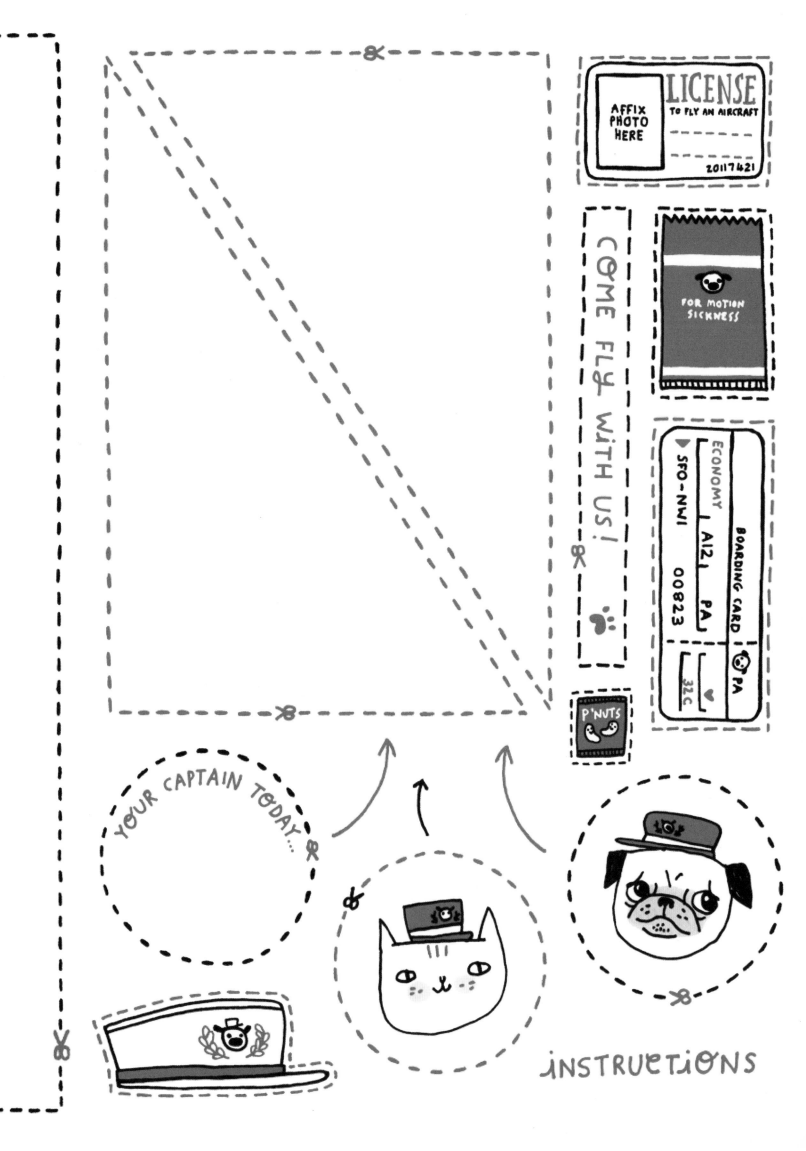

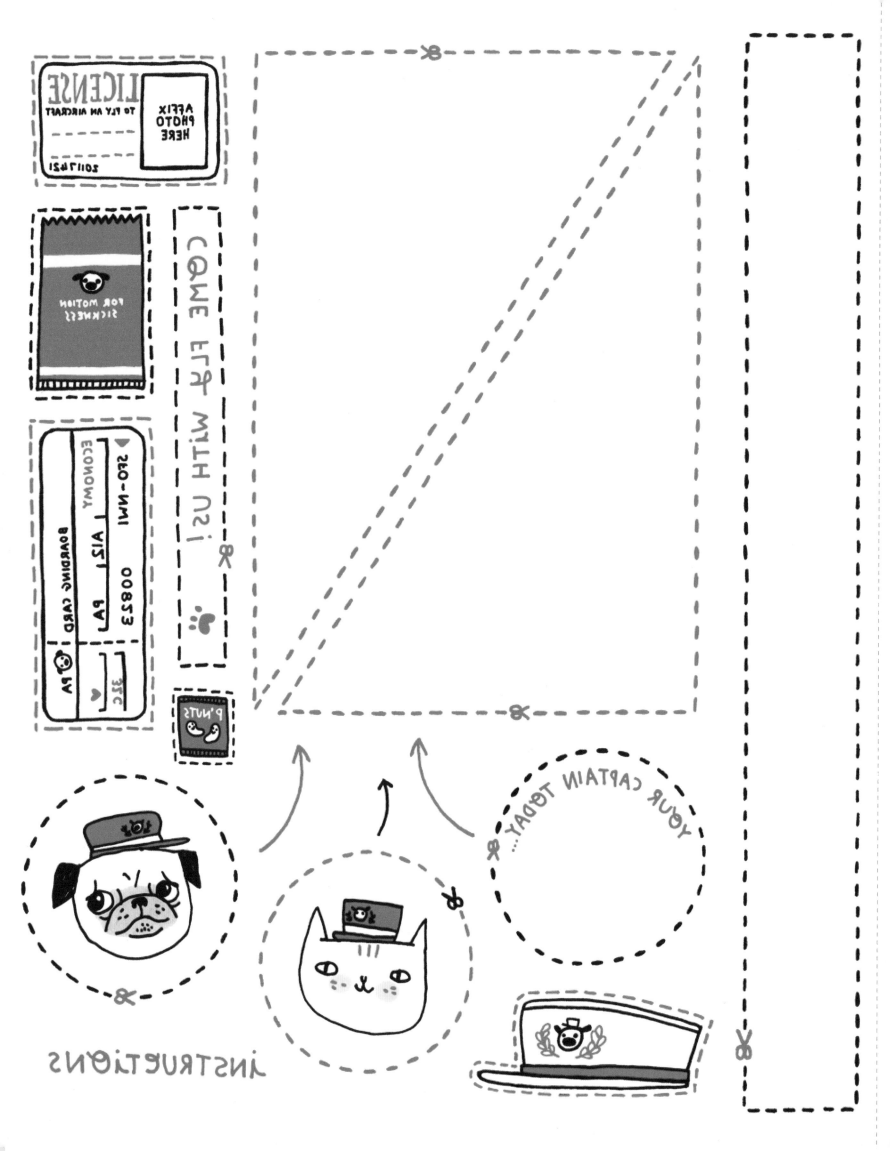

RUSSELL
LENG

Russell Leng is an artist living in Vancouver, Canada, who holds a BA in art from Trinity Western University. Being interested in the relationship between natural and built environments, his time is often spent daydreaming about cabins, neon lights, and the feeling he gets while hearing the ocean before seeing it. Visit his website at Russellleng.com.

Artists get their starts in a myriad of ways: some planned, some completely accidental, with purpose, or with no sense of why the hand insists on moving. When did you realize you were making art for the first time? How did it feel?

My older brother and his friends were usually pretty kind to me growing up, but he had this one friend Carl who loved picking on me. I remember one day after school when Carl was over, the two of them convinced me to crawl underneath the stairs with them. I must have pushed their buttons or provoked them in some way because they ended up tying me up so I couldn't move. I was stuck underneath the stairs, trapped in a dark corner for what seemed to be hours. My hands were tied behind my back, and the door was locked. I started to imagine my mom shoving food underneath the door so I could survive in my claustrophobic cave of humiliation. Just as I was about to scream for help, I noticed a black marker lying on the cold concrete ground beside me. With my hands tied behind my back, I had nothing else to do but draw on the concrete wall I was sitting against. Though my wrists were tied together, my fingers were nimble enough to grab the marker and draw. Suddenly all of my anger at Carl and my brother was lost as I drew pictures of shapes, wrote secret codes, and calmed myself down by making art.

SUPPLIES

Pattern, provided, or
one 8½-by-11-inch sheet of paper

Scissors

Pen or pencil

Clear tape

Rubber band

INSTRUCTIONS

When I was around ten years old, my friends and I used to make these things called "butt-wads." They were like paper planes in that we used them to pass notes, get the attention of the girls we liked, and to annoy each other at recess.

1 Cut out the pattern, or tear a sheet of paper into 8½-by-2½-inch strips. I recommend writing a secret on the paper, then rolling it up as tight as you can.

2 After you have a tightly rolled cylinder, color or mark the ends so that your butt-wads can be indentified from those of your classmates/colleagues/cousins/inmates/roommates, et cetera.

3 Next, wrap the paper with clear tape, and bend at the middle so that the butt-wad resembles a "V."

4 In one hand, loop a rubber band around your index finger and thumb. In the other hand place the paper "V" in front of the elastic and pull back. Watch your new little paper plane soar through the air.

5 Gather your paper plane and repeat.